MOUNTAIN GORILLA

CONTENTS

© Aladdin Books Ltd 1989

Designed and produced by
Aladdin Books Ltd
70 Old Compton Street
London W1

*First published in the
United States in 1989 by*
Gloucester Press
387 Park Avenue South
New York, NY 10016

ISBN 0-531–17179-5

Library of Congress Catalog
Card Number: 89-50447

Design Rob Hillier, Andy Wilkinson
Editor Julia Slater
Researcher Cecilia Weston-Baker
Illustrator Ron Hayward Associates

Printed in Belgium

PROJECT WILDLIFE

MOUNTAIN GORILLA

Michael Bright

Gloucester Press
New York : London : Toronto : Sydney

Introduction

The mountain gorilla is one of man's closest relatives and the largest living primate. Scientists discovered the species in 1902. Early explorers traveling in the tropical forests of West Africa brought back stories of the gorilla attacking and killing people. It became a symbol of all that is powerful and dangerous in the jungle. Movies such as *King Kong* (1933) focused on the supposedly violent nature of the gorilla. But in reality the gorilla is far from being a savage beast. It is a gentle and shy creature. It hides in the forest, lives a peaceful family life and avoids any conflict with people.

However, human contact with the mountain gorilla has been less than gentle. Much of the forest upon which it depends for food and shelter has been cut down. Recent counts show that there are fewer than 400 mountain gorillas remaining because their habitat has been partially destroyed. With so few individuals left, the species can be considered a prime candidate for extinction.

▽ A mountain gorilla sits in its shrinking forest home.

Gorilla distribution

Gorillas are only found in the wild in Africa. Three subspecies of gorilla exist: the mountain gorilla, the western lowland gorilla, and the eastern lowland gorilla. The mountain gorilla is black with long hair and is often seen in wildlife movies and television programs. About 400 live in a small area of bamboo and mountain forests on the slopes of the Virunga Volcanos in Rwanda, Zaire and Uganda. They are the rarest of the three subspecies.

The lowland gorillas have short hair and are those seen in zoos. Approximately 40,000 western lowland gorillas still survive in the tropical rain forests of Gabon, Equatorial Guinea, Cameroon, and the Congo, with a small isolated population in Nigeria. Some 4,000 eastern lowland gorillas inhabit the forests of Eastern Zaire. The lowland gorillas' habitat is also threatened.

▷ The map shows the three main gorilla populations. Gorillas do not leave the forest and do not swim. This means the eastern race is trapped between the Great Rift Valley and the Congo River. The ancestors of the western lowland gorillas, however, may have migrated from East Africa via ancient forests in the highlands of the Central African Republic, to settle in West Africa.

▽ The enlarged map shows the six active volcanoes on which the mountain gorillas live. It also shows a conservation problem – they live in an area belonging to three nations.

▽ Mt. Visoke is home to mountain gorillas.

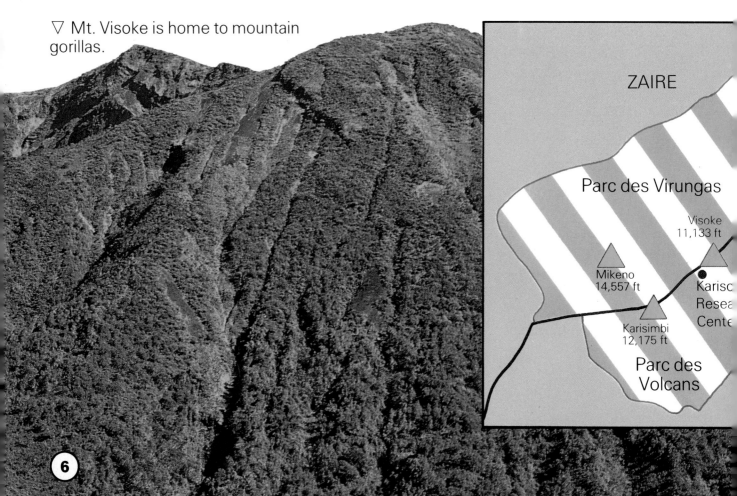

ZAIRE

Parc des Virungas

Visoke
11,133 ft

Mikeno
14,557 ft

Karisc
Resea
Cente

Karisimbi
12,175 ft

Parc des
Volcans

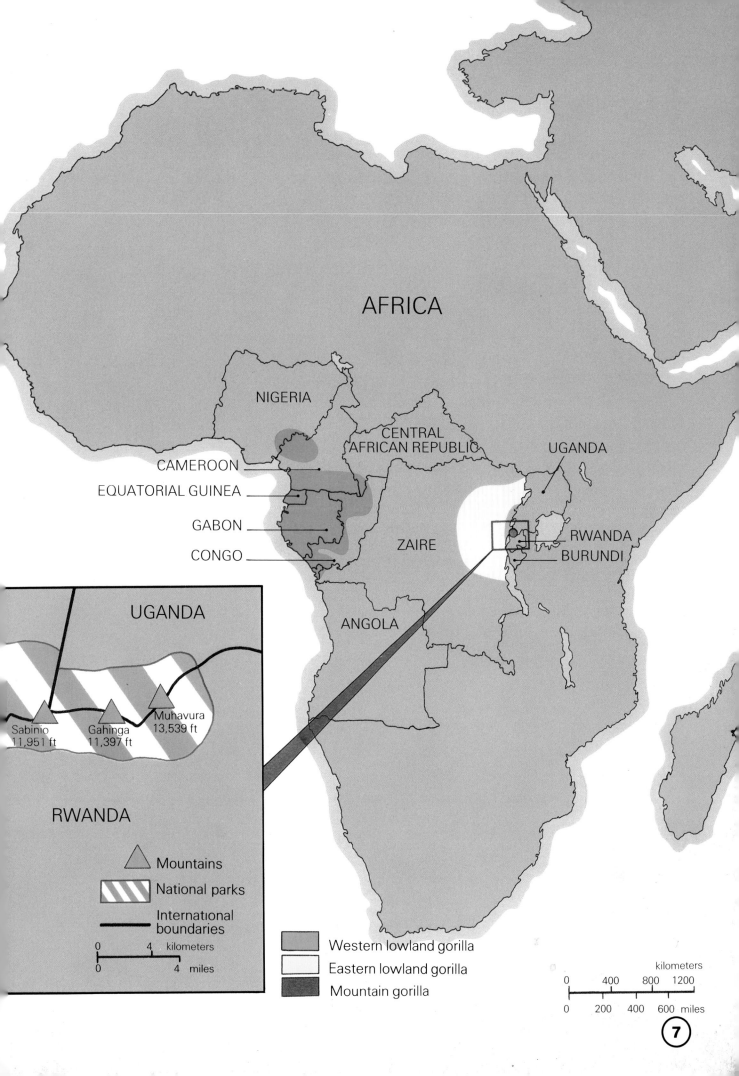

AFRICA

NIGERIA

CENTRAL
AFRICAN REPUBLIC

UGANDA

CAMEROON

EQUATORIAL GUINEA

GABON

CONGO

ZAIRE

RWANDA

BURUNDI

ANGOLA

UGANDA

Sabinio
11,951 ft

Gahinga
11,397 ft

Muhavura
13,539 ft

RWANDA

△ Mountains

National parks

International
boundaries

0   4   kilometers

0   4   miles

Western lowland gorilla

Eastern lowland gorilla

Mountain gorilla

kilometers

0   400   800   1200

0   200   400   600 miles

7

The capture and killing of gorillas

Mountain gorillas are slaughtered deliberately for a rather sinister souvenir trade. Adult gorillas are found with their heads and hands missing. Sometimes they are killed accidentally in the traps that poachers set for antelope. Usually the gorilla's wrists or heels are caught in the wire or hemp snare. If it cannot get free the animal will be in agony for many hours until it succumbs to starvation. If the gorilla escapes, its wound becomes infected and the animal will eventually die a slow and painful death. Poachers helped to reduce the Virunga mountain gorilla population from about 500 in 1960 to 240 in 1980.

An entire family of lowland gorillas may be slain in order to capture a youngster and sell it illegally to a private animal collection, a zoo, or a laboratory for human medical research. In some areas, lowland gorillas are killed because they are considered a crop pest. Many are butchered for food.

△ This gorilla has lost its hand. At least two others in Rwanda have survived amputations in snares.

▷ A male gorilla defends his family with a mock charge: he will even run straight onto a poacher's spear.

"We found [the gorilla, Digit] speared, headless and handless. It is probably the worst experience you can have to see someone, not something, someone you know in that condition."

Ian Redmond, Gorilla researcher

The gorilla trade

Foreign tourists visiting Africa have been taking home gruesome curios. Gorilla hands and feet have been sold for about $22 each as novelty ashtrays. Gorilla teeth are used to make "ethnic" jewelry and other ornaments. Their heads are stuffed and sold to those who wish to display them alongside other "trophies." Gorilla skulls are cleaned and sold as macabre ornaments. During one year 30 skulls intended for foreign buyers were discovered in poachers' camps. Locally, poachers sell ears, tongues, genitals and small fingers to witch doctors to make a potion that is supposed to endow the recipient with the strength of a gorilla.

The trade is illegal. Any nation which has signed the Convention of International Trade in Endangered Species of Wild Fauna and Flora (CITES) should not be trading in gorillas or parts of gorillas. Nevertheless, tourists browsing through marketplaces are shown and invited to buy gorilla souvenirs.

△ The amulet in the picture above is decorated with shells and the teeth of a gorilla.

△ This baby mountain gorilla was saved from poachers. But it died soon after the frightening ordeal of being orphaned and captured.

◁ A cache of macabre souvenirs confiscated by the Rwandan authorities. The poachers bury the skulls so the police won't find them.

In 1976, 497 gorillas were known to be living in captivity. Of those, 402 were taken from the wild, most coming from Cameroon in West Africa. Today, the trade is illegal. All countries with wild gorillas have protection laws. Yet, animal dealers still can get over $75,000 for a gorilla. Capturing a baby gorilla means having to shoot its mother and others in its family. Tragically, baby mountain gorillas do not survive long after separation from their group.

Habitat destruction

The mountain gorillas' home has been gradually taken away from them. As more and more people need space in which to live, they are chopping down the mountain forests. This forest destruction was once the major cause of the reduction in gorilla numbers. In Rwanda, for example, the human population is rapidly expanding. People need to cut down the trees and bamboo to build their homes. They must also clear land so they can graze cattle and grow their crops.

Yet, cattle have grazed right up to the mountain slopes and have moved into what was once gorilla country. Gorillas are shy animals and are disturbed by human activities. So, as more and more people and their cattle encroached on the mountains, the places where gorillas could wander and forage undisturbed got smaller. Without the protection they now receive, the gorillas would have nowhere to live.

△ To build this house, the farmer may be tempted to illegally cut bamboo in the national park.

Herds of cattle that once △ grazed in gorilla country are now excluded from the park in Rwanda.

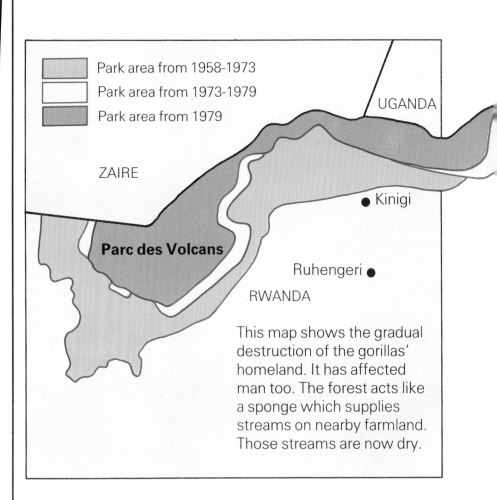

Park area from 1958-1973
Park area from 1973-1979
Park area from 1979

UGANDA

ZAIRE

Kinigi

Parc des Volcans

Ruhengeri

RWANDA

This map shows the gradual destruction of the gorillas' homeland. It has affected man too. The forest acts like a sponge which supplies streams on nearby farmland. Those streams are now dry.

The most extensive forest destruction in Rwanda occurred in 1969 when 40 percent of the national park in which the gorillas live was given over to cultivation. Farmers began planting pyrethrum, a daisy-like flower from which an insecticide is made. It was grown to replace DDT and other pesticides dangerous to wildlife. But in Rwanda, pyrethrum itself became the greatest threat to the gorillas.

Today, pyrethrum is made synthetically in the laboratory. But this move has come too late to save much of the gorillas' land. The forest has already been destroyed, and the land now supports many people living outside the park, some of whom enter illegally to hunt, gather wood, set traps, and collect honey.

The fight against poaching

In recent years, anti-poaching patrols on the Rwandan side of the border have considerably reduced the killing of adult gorillas and the smuggling of babies. Six patrols, each with four to six men, comb the mountain forest to look for signs of poachers. Each ranger finding a wire or hemp snare gets paid a bonus. Often the rangers find 100 traps in a day. They have removed many thousands of snares and traps and caught many poachers who were put in jail and out of business.

However, the national park is difficult to patrol. It is over 60 km (37 mi) long and just 2 km (1.2 mi) wide in places. Furthermore, it runs along the frontier of three nations. Poachers can enter the national park land from Zaire or Uganda, cross to Rwanda to set their traps, collect their booty of antelope and buffalo, and quickly escape back across the border. The mountainous terrain and thick foliage makes it hard for anti-poaching patrols to catch them.

△ An anti-poaching patrol removes a wire and bamboo spring snare.

▽ National park guards have tracked down and arrested a poacher.

The Mountain Gorilla Project

During the 1970s poachers killed so many gorillas that there was great concern about this fast disappearing species. So, in 1978 the Mountain Gorilla Project (MGP) was set up in an attempt to save the mountain gorillas from extinction. The MGP works with the Rwandan government and provides equipment, training, and advice for anti-poaching patrols. It has also started an education program that helps teach local people about the value of their gorillas and other wildlife.

▽ Dian Fossey, watching a large male gorilla. Fossey was known locally as "Nyiramachabelli" which means "the old lady who lives alone in the forest without a man." She dedicated her life to saving and studying the mountain gorillas. She died in 1985, murdered by poachers or by those opposed to preserving the national park.

▽ Funds from wildlife charities worldwide also support the study of gorillas in the wild. Ian Redmond, the British researcher seen below, grooms a male gorilla while looking for parasites. It is important to keep a close scientific and medical eye on the gorillas as they are susceptible to many diseases such as measles, pneumonia, meningitis and internal gut parasites.

the Digit Fund

◁ The Digit Fund helps pay for park patrols.

American researcher Dian Fossey pioneered the study of gorillas in the wild. In December 1977, poachers killed her favorite male gorilla known as Digit. He was found with his head and hands missing and numerous spearwounds in his chest. He had died defending his group from poachers. In his memory, the Digit Fund was set up to help gorilla research and conservation in Rwanda. Inspired by the successses of MGP and the Digit Fund, similar projects have started in Zaire and Uganda.

Reserves and research

The mountain gorillas live in Africa's oldest national park, originally called Albert National Park. It was established in 1925 specifically to protect the gorillas of the Virunga Mountains. The area is now split between three countries – Rwanda, Zaire and Uganda. In Rwanda the gorillas living in the Parc des Volcans are relatively safe for the present. However, in Zaire's Virunga National Park and in Uganda's Bwindi Forest Reserve, guards have been beaten up by heavily armed poachers.

Yet, reserves are not enough to save the gorilla. It is also important to learn more about them so we are better able to help them. Gorillas are understandably wary of people. In order for scientists to carry out research, gorilla groups must get used to having humans watch them. This process is called "habituation." Scientists at the Karisoke Research Center, by Rwanda's Mt. Visoke, have habituated several gorilla groups and have been observing their life almost every day for more than twenty years.

▷ The small corrugated metal cabin in the photograph was Dian Fossey's first cabin in Rwanda and the first permanent building of the Karisoke Research Center. It was established at 4:30 pm on September 24, 1967, after a five hour climb from the lowland. It is situated between Mt. Visoke and Mt. Karisimbi in the Parc des Volcans in Rwanda. It rains there a lot and the area is frequently fog-bound.

▽ This large adult male gorilla dwarfs the tracker who has been following his group. The man must not look the gorilla in the eye and must not make any sudden moves. By observing gorilla etiquette, researchers can stay with a group for most of the day.

"If we don't act to protect the mountain gorilla and its habitat, then everyone will lose in the long term — even the local people — when the deforested slopes suffer erosion."

Dr Alan Goodall, Director of the Karisoke Research Center.

Gorilla watching in the wild

Rwanda has become the gorilla capital of the world. In 1979, just 1,788 tourists visited Rwanda as a whole. In 1987, 4,500 people came for the gorillas alone, and that number is likely to increase after the impact of the feature film "Gorillas in the Mist." A two to three hour trek in the Virunga Mountains and a one hour encounter with a group of mountain gorillas costs about $175 per person.

Rwanda is a poor country and must make the best use of the resources it possesses. The park and its gorillas must compete with those who would like to use the land for other purposes such as farming. But the Rwandan government has realized that the gorillas themselves are valuable. Consequently, the gorillas pay their own way by attracting tourists to visit them.

Four gorilla groups let visitors come near them for about one hour each day. The visitors can sometimes see over 60 animals in all. These are truly wild gorillas. They are not tame. Often, they are intensely inquisitive about their human cousins – they have been known to come up to the camera and inspect it when photographers are out filming.

△ These tourists are on their way to see the mountain gorillas. There is no guarantee that they will find a group. If the gorillas do not want to be disturbed they simply disappear into the dense, almost magical, mountain forests.

Disturbance of gorilla groups is kept to a minimum. Only six people accompanied by guides are allowed to visit at any one time. The trek up the volcano slopes, with giant stinging nettles and other dangers along the route, is often long and difficult. It may take two hours or more to find the gorillas. Furthermore, if the gorillas become agitated the humans must go back. Most tourists say that being face to face with a wild gorilla is the most exciting experience they have ever had.

△ These fortunate visitors will have flown to Kigali (the capital of Rwanda), driven for 5 hours along the mountain highway to Ruhengeri (the nearest town to the Parc des Volcans), bumped over six miles of rough terrain and climbed for several hours up steep mountain slopes – probably in the pouring rain.

Gorillas in zoos

All of the gorillas found in zoos are lowland ones since mountain gorillas have never survived long in zoos. At one time zoo gorillas were taken from the wild, but now most are bred in captivity. Unscrupulous zoos, however, still try to obtain them from animal dealers, who buy from poachers. They find ways to bypass the authorities. Some claim that babies, orphaned when their mothers were killed for food, should be taken into the safety of a zoo. But this encourages an illegal trade as poachers realize that zoos will still take in wild gorillas. To stop this, gorilla researchers are trying to set up a sanctuary in West Africa where they will teach orphaned gorillas how to survive in the wild.

Some zoos are preferable to others. In the better zoos, the gorillas live in compounds where they can move about and forage as they would naturally. In the worst zoos, the gorillas live on concrete. Nevertheless, lowland gorillas bred in zoos are a safeguard against extinction should anything happen to those living in the wild.

Kiki, the gorilla in the photograph on the left, swapped his concrete cage for a new "natural" enclosure at Seattle's Woodland Park Zoo and appeared much happier. Gorillas, like the one below, spend a lot of time just sitting and staring, whether in a zoo or in the wild. But if they have nowhere to forage, they get bored and show signs of abnormal behavior.

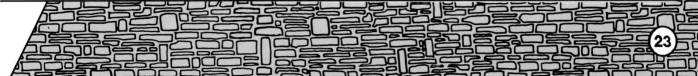

The mountain gorilla's future

Conservationists are feeling cautiously optimistic about the future of the mountain gorillas. Rwanda, Zaire and Uganda have realized the importance of protecting them. Tourist dollars have underlined their value, particularly to the local peoples. More effective anti-poaching patrols have brought about a noticeable reduction in the number of animals slaughtered. As a consequence gorilla numbers are beginning to increase. During the 1980s, for instance, the number of mountain gorillas living in the Virunga Mountains rose by approximately ten percent.

▽ This mother and baby are still in danger. Recently six gorillas died from diseases possibly brought in by tourists. One major epidemic of a killer disease could wipe out the entire population. In order to keep a watch on the health of these rare animals the Morris Animal Foundation of the United States is funding a veterinary center in Rwanda that will provide emergency care for wild animals.

"We're still dealing with a very shaky situation but I think it's fairly safe to say now that the mountain gorilla is going to accompany us into the twenty-first century."

Craig Sholley, Director of the Mountain Gorilla Project.

The overpopulation problem is not disappearing. Rwanda, with 4.7 million people living in a space the size of Maryland, is Africa's most densely populated country. Its population is expected to double before the next century.

Each year 23,000 new families require plots of land on which to live and grow crops. Every new farm brings greater pressure to bear on the gorillas' remote mountain home. If encroachment into the Virunga Mountains is not checked it is possible that the mountain gorilla will be an animal that was discovered and became extinct in the same century.

These children are about to see a movie about the mountain gorillas. Education is vital to gorilla conservation.

Gorilla fact file 1

Gorillas live in groups that may stay together for many years. On average each group consists of three adult females, four or five offspring of various ages and one dominant adult male. He is known as the silverback on account of his silver-colored saddle. He leads the group and defends it against intruders.

Range

Gorillas do not travel far. Although they are surrounded by their mainly vegetarian food, they must find time to forage and digest it. So, they travel less than a mile per day and rest frequently. A group's home range may be 13 to 19 square miles, and the home ranges of several groups may overlap. As they are not aggressive animals they avoid fighting for territory.

A mountain gorilla group does not strip all the vegetation away from an eating site before moving on to the next one. Instead, the gorillas will eat a certain amount of foliage from one spot and then they will forage somewhere else. In this way, they leave behind plenty of shoots that can grow up again. This ensures that there is another crop of fresh food available for them the next time they pass through.

Body

Mountain gorillas are big and powerful animals. A silverback can stand up to almost 6 ft tall and weigh 396 lbs. Much of its bulk is muscle. Females are smaller. They can be almost 5 ft tall and weigh 198 lbs.

Gorillas walk on all fours and are known as "knuckle-walkers." They rest their weight on the backs of the middle joints of the second to fifth fingers. There the skin is thickened.

Skull and brain

The gorilla skull is massive. Adult males have a crest on top to which are anchored the muscles that operate powerful jaws. The gorilla's brain is much smaller in relation to its body size than that of humans.

Teeth

Gorillas have very large molar teeth to grind up their fibrous vegetable diet.

Hands and feet

Gorilla hands are broad with an opposable thumb. They can manipulate the smallest of twigs. Their feet are adapted for life on the ground and their toes are almost in a line like those of humans.

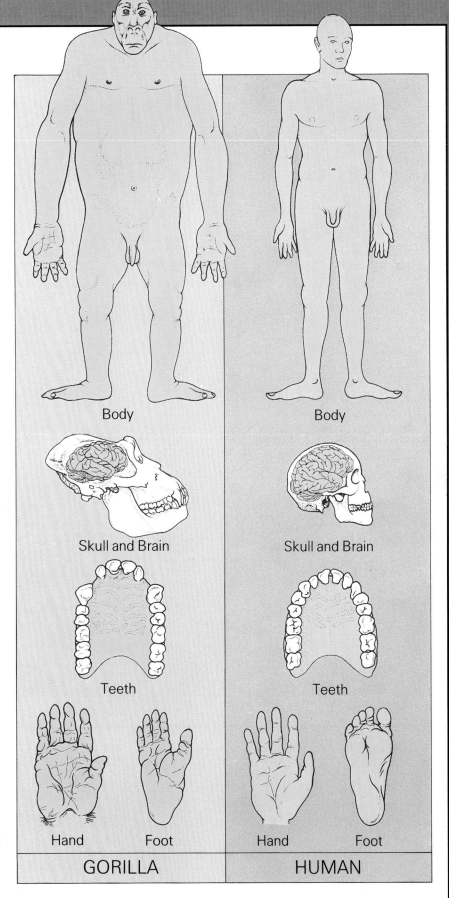

Body

Skull and Brain

Teeth

Hand   Foot

GORILLA

Body

Skull and Brain

Teeth

Hand   Foot

HUMAN

Gorilla fact file 2

Daily life

Mountain gorillas wake up just after dawn. If it is sunny or if there was heavy rain in the night they may sleep a bit later. During the morning they feed, and then take a nap at about noon.

While the young animals continue to play, some adults construct day nests and rest. Others just sit around or groom each other. In the afternoon, another bout of foraging and feeding ends at about 6 pm with nest building and then sleep. A group may move on while foraging, with more travel in the afternoon than in the morning. In heavy rain, the gorillas stop feeding, sit on their haunches, with their arms folded, and receive a thorough soaking.

Nests

At night gorillas sleep in nests. These are platforms built of branches and leaves. Each gorilla bends and twists vegetation, folding it in a circle under its body. This is how it keeps its body away from the cold and damp ground.

When a gorilla sleeps it may lie on its side with its legs drawn up to the body or on its tummy with its legs tucked underneath. Nests made on or near the ground take a few minutes to make, whereas those in the forks of trees take longer.

Foraging and Food

Gorillas may grab a snack while on the move or else enjoy a proper sit-down meal. They reach out in all directions sometimes chewing on one handful while grabbing for the next.

In general, mountain gorillas eat shoots, leaves, and stems. Occasionally a few slugs and grubs find their way into the diet. About two percent of their diet is fruit. Some plants are preferred only at particular times of year. For example, in spring when the bamboo begins to grow, some gorilla groups come down the mountains to feed on the shoots.

Sometimes gorillas eat soil. They seek out earth rich in calcium and potassium. In one place on Mt. Visoke, the gorillas have excavated such large holes beneath some tree roots that they have dug their own large caverns.

Food

Mountain gorillas usually eat a common vine called "gallium," but they are partial to wild celery, stinging nettles, thistles, bamboo, and more than 50 other plant species. Special delicacies include a shelf-like bracket fungus, a high altitude relative of mistletoe.

Gorilla fact file 3

The most well-known gorilla display is chest beating. This is one in a series of events — hooting, pretend feeding, standing upright, throwing vegetation and chest beating.

The display lasts for about half a minute. The chest beating sounds are made by slapping the cupped hands on the chest. It is prompted by many different situations.

All animals in a group may beat their chests. It says "I'm over here and I am nervous or excited about something." Only males perform the whole display.

◁ The way a silverback (adult male) stands, sits or stares can convey an enormous amount of information to the rest of the group. His very presence during a squabble between adolescents can bring them into line.

Courtship
There is no breeding season in the Virunga Mountains. Gorillas can mate at any time of the year. Females begin to breed at about age 10. Males mature a little later, but competition for females is so intense that a male might not mate until he is 20 years old. The dominant silverback has sole rights to mate with the mature females in his group.

Young

Most births occur at night in the mother's night nest. A baby gorilla weighs about 4½ lbs at birth and it has little fur on its pinkish-grey skin. It crawls on its belly at nine weeks, and walks on two legs by 12 months. It is weaned at 2½-3 years. About 40 percent of babies die before age three. The survivors receive lots of care from their parents. The mother gorilla carries her infant below her tummy at first, but later it rides on her back. During the day, an "aunty" might look after the infants while the mothers feed nearby. Playtime is usually during the midday rest period, when the youngsters chase, wrestle and mock-bite each other.

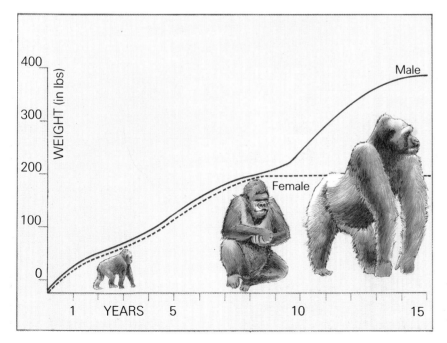

Growing up

Silverbacks acquire their silvery hair at age 12 and may leave the group and travel alone until they find an area where they can live and attract their own females. They are not driven away but leave of their own accord. Aggressive behavior only occurs when a lone male challenges a mature silverback for the leadership of an established group. Young females may leave for a smaller group or join a lone male to start a new family.

Index

Photographic Credits:
Cover and pages 8, 12, 13, 14, 15, 16, 18, 19,
20, 21, 22, 25, 26, 28 and 31: Ian Redmond;
pages 4-5, 6, 9, 17, 22-23, 24 and 30: Bruce
Coleman Ltd; page 29: Planet Earth.

To find out more about mountain gorilla
conservation and research, please send a
self-addressed stamped envelope to:
The Digit Fund, 45 Inverness Drive East,
Englewood, CO 80112-5480

PRINTED IN BELGIUM BY
proost
INTERNATIONAL BOOK PRODUCTION